A BLACK DEMAND
FOR
POLICE REFORM

A New Paradigm

By

Ozie Lee Hall, Jr.

Advanced Education Systems Publishing

Spring Lake, NC   28390

Library of Congress: Case No. 1-9160217871

Advanced Education System Publishing
Publisher
P.O. Box 387
Spring Lake, NC   28390

ISBN: 9798679030220

DEDICATION

This book is dedicated to my children and grandchildren and the families of America whom will be impacted by future police policies, and to the mothers, grandmothers, and sisters who now fear every time their sons go out that they may become the next victim of police violence or murder.

CONTENTS

PREFACE

If you go out on the streets of most Black communities in the United States and randomly interview Black males over age 18, at least nine out of ten can relate a personal experience of being racially profiled, experiencing or witnessing another Black man being harassed and abused by police, or being impacted in some way by police misconduct. Cellphone cameras have enabled citizens to capture the Black male experience on video and confirmed what Black people have been saying for many years. The truth is that the history of American policing goes back to the slave catchers whose job was to hunt down runaway slaves.

After the civil war (1861-1865), states passed laws which criminalized the poverty conditions of the newly freed slaves. Ultimately, the police became an occupying force to control Black communities by fear and intimidation of Black citizens. Police agencies were racially segregated. Vestiges of racial segregation remain in police departments across the United States today.

Systemic racism continues to plague police operations and filters down to police officers on the streets who abuse Black citizens. The conservative sees nothing wrong with the conduct of police in Black communities and labels people who protest police misconduct as criminals. On the other hand, a majority of Americans have seen cellphone videos showing police misconduct which cannot be easily explained away. America is at a crossroads. Many citizens are demanding police reform and that abuse of Black citizens stop. Many conservatives call for law and order and to crackdown on protest but fail to acknowledge a need for reform.

Conservatives claim that policing is a very dangerous job and they support giving police broad discretion in their use of force against citizens, particularly Black citizens. Conservatives support police being immune from prosecution for misconduct. The truth is that in the United States being a police officer is a safer job than being a construction laborer, a farmer, or a nursing assistant. America must grow beyond her ugly past. The standards of police professional responsibility must be raised to new levels. We must demand more of police. It is time to change how police agencies operate in the United States.

The purpose of this book is to start a discussion about police reform. Many Americans argue in desperation that police agencies should be defunded as a means to force reforms. Others argue that all police agencies should be abolished, all police fired, and then create new police type agencies to hire back some officers and weed out the corruption and racism which exist in the current system. Still others say the existing system can be reformed by retraining police officers, implementing new programs, setting new policies, and eliminating police unions.

The United States arrests and imprisons more of its citizens than the supposed most repressive nations in the world. Recent studies of the City of Ferguson and over 100 U.S. cities show that police willfully, maliciously, and intentionally target and racially profile Black communities for the purpose of extracting revenue in the form of fines and fees and to attract federal funding as the result of high crime rates associated with racially targeted arrest. Prosecutors and the Courts have been shown to work in cooperation with local police to support this systemically racist system.

Perhaps it's not too late to reform the system and stop the continued economic exploitation of Black Americans. Black America has suffered economic exploitation in America beginning with slavery. Economic exploitation just transformed after slavery and has continued to evolve and become more sophisticated. The Black community has become a permanent economic underclass in America without Reparation or compensation for historic economic exploitation.

The issue of Reparations for Black American descendants of slaves, victims of Jim Crow, and current discrimination practices is tied directly to the discussion of police reform. Police reform must be a part of Reparations to Black Americans. The late Rev. Dr. Martin Luther King, Jr. once said of the Black community in the United States that "our destiny is tied up with the destiny of America."

Black people cannot continue to be exploited economically and abused by the police without consequences. We all should be able to live in harmony and peace, but if not, the future is uncertain. Choose reform because it is the right thing to do for everyone.

INTRODUCTION

In 1988, the author visited Japan as part of a U.S. Delegation organized by the Milton S. Eisenhower Foundation. The Delegation included high-ranking U.S. police officials from multiple jurisdictions including Wilmington (Delaware), Philadelphia, New York, Washington, D.C., Baltimore, Atlanta, Portland, Houston, Albuquerque, and Los Angeles. The Delegation also included community organization leaders from each jurisdiction who managed children and youth services agencies dedicated to steering children and youth away from a life of crime and toward a path of progressive progress. The author was the community organization representative from Wilmington, Delaware. Wilmington City Police Community Services Director, Pete Hickman, was the police official on the Delegation from Wilmington, Delaware.

The Delegation's mission was to investigate why Japan, at the time, a nation with a population which was half the size of the United States occupying a land space about the size of the State of California had one of the lowest crime rates in the world and practically no police brutality or corruption. We wanted to understand why Japan had only about 40,000 people in jails and prisons nationwide. At the time, the United States had over 2 million people incarcerated in jails and prisons and nearly 5 million people on probation and parole. Before we began our 13-hour flight from Los Angeles to Tokyo we participated in a workshop with Professor David H. Bayley the author of the book "Forces of Order." Professor Bayley provided us a briefing on the findings of his research on policing in Japan and its contrast to police practices in the United States.

When the Delegation arrived in Tokyo we were hosted by the Japanese National Police Agency and Tokyo Metropolitan Police Agency. We visited the Japanese National Police Academy, did ride-a-longs with rank and file police officers, meet with citizens neighborhood crime association groups, and participated in multiple briefings and information exchange sessions which enabled us to develop an independent view of what was happening on the ground in Japan which made them different and so successful with its police practices in Japan.

The community organization representatives debated among themselves about whether what we were seeing in Japan could be replicated in the United States. The central issue which kept coming up was whether the existence of systemic racism which has deep historical roots in the United States was a barrier to police reform. Some of us discussed our analysis of the fundamental problems in the United States and what it would take to bring about genuine police reform in the United States. Even then, we recognized that U.S. police reform would require a major transformation in thinking which would require a major transformation in police leadership across the United States. In 1988, a major transformation in police leadership thinking was unlikely. In 2020, the author believes conditions are ripe to reopen and expand the discussion of police reform. Not only is police reform necessary, but the future of our nation depends on it.

Police corruption, police brutality, the open murder of citizens by police, and the failures of our system of accountability has strained police community relations to its limits. Police reform is needed now.

The Japanese police system was driven by crime prevention while in the United States its was driven by arrest and incarceration of citizens. Japanese police officers were required to complete two years of police training which included character development activities and trainings which help police officers become effective leaders in the communities to which they are assigned and required to live. In the United States, Basic Law Enforcement Training take about 6 months and police training curriculums unwittingly exacerbate police brutality and corruption. In addition, the police union structure in the United States has resulted in police leadership which polarizes police from communities and have created a culture of police corruption and lack of accountability.

The relationship between police and many communities in the United States have become so strained of recent that many citizens have called for "Defunding the Police." This call to defund the police is a desperate call for change after U.S. citizens watched a cell phone video of a police officer murder a Black man by putting his knee on the man's neck for 8 minutes and 46 seconds as the man repeatedly told offices he could not breath and cried out to his deceased Mother before he died. Several other police officers stood by and watched this blatant murder without intervening. This murder is not an isolated incident. It followed a long string of open murders and executions of citizens by police across the United States.

As a nation, we have reached the bottom. We must change and reform. This book is written to help us begin the process of major reform.

POLICE/COMMUNITY RELATIONS

Many community groups have argued for the creation of Police Review Boards, Citizen Review Boards, and many other ways to seek to establish police accountability. These systems have not worked or have had only marginal impact. The major problem is almost always a lack of real authority to implement meaningful change. The Japanese model which is crime prevention driven and where police officers actively assist local communities build its response to crime is an enlightened police/community relations model.

Local communities in the United States are often suffering in poverty. In Japan, the average Japanese household in 1988 have an average saving of $30,000.00. The author is an advocate of Reparations for Black Americans. We must address the role and impact of poverty on crime in the Black community and throughout the United States in general. The Black community has historically been economically exploited in the United States. Reparations is an issue which must ultimately be addressed.

The issue of police/community relations in Japan has been described by saying "the people control themselves." "The people practice self-discipline." This is a distinguishing characteristic of Japanese culture. The United States is not built upon some deep-rooted historic culture. America is a relatively new nation which contains a mixture of cultures, ethnicities, and traditions.

The United States presents major differences from Japan which impact police/community relations. Japan is a homogenous culture. The diversity in the United States requires that police officers develop the ability to transcend the restriction of their own personal culture background and present as a unifying force in American society. The police cannot do this if they are a bunch of miseducated misfits.

Police are the police for everyone. Police officers cannot treat each group differently or based upon their own cultural, ethnic, or racial bias and maintain any level of credibility. Ruling by force is also not a viable option. Diversity in the United States presents unique opportunities for American Democracy. We are interconnected to people all over the globe. We set the example for the rest of the world.

When police engage in misconduct and the world witnesses American police violate the civil rights and human rights of American citizens, we lose moral authority in the world and our global position is weakened.

Law enforcement leaders should never take positive police/community relations for granted or disregard its importance. A single corrupt act or brutality by police and the system's response to it can easily erupt into protest, burning of property, looting, and major destruction of property. It could also lead to strategically targeted violence against the police and government officials.

Law enforcement officials should be mindful and remain vigilant to assure the police and the community are working together and not antagonistic to each other. Police must be a part of the community. It won't work if police officers are racist, labor under stereotypes, and act against the interest of the community.

When police kill its own citizens eventually the citizens will protect themselves from the police. Totalitarian governments cannot last because the people have a greater capacity to implement violence than the police when pressed. The better solution is to establish positive police/community relations.

The people must lead on the issue of crime in the community. Crime occurs in communities within the midst of the people. The people witness crime. A well-organized community determines what is a crime and has the capacity to regulate crime. The police are simply an enforcement tool of the community.

In the United States, the police have become a tool of the upper classes and powerful political groups. The police are used to suppress the poor and Black communities and uphold the current system of economic exploitation.

American society has created a system to manufacture crime in poor and Black communities. Black communities have been historically locked out of the mainstream of society. The Black communities are redlined by Banks and Financial Institutions where money is extracted from the community, but little put back in. Black communities pay higher insurance rates, we pay higher rates for food, clothing, and shelter. We are targeted by police and racially profiled to extract fines and fees. We are denied access to high quality education. We are discriminated against in employment opportunities. We experience a major wealth gap as compared to the white community. This is all part of a system of exploitation which began with the trans-Atlantic slave trade.

A new social contract is needed between the Black community and America. We cannot continue down this path. Positive police/community relations is essential to the continued existence of the United States as a nation.

We can eliminate crime in our communities when we have equal employment and pay, access to improved housing, end redlining of Black communities, stop insurance exploitation, and end racial profiling.

When young Black children see white police officers come into Black communities and threaten and harass Black youth and Black men and see the police commit crimes against Black people that go unpunished it pushes them on a path toward crime. It makes them lose respect for the law and the system as a whole. Black youth, in despair, take matters into their own hands. Often the result is getting caught up in a system that ruins their lives and is damaging to the community.

If you grow up in a community in poverty, receive a poor quality of education from racist teachers, and your community offers you no hope your life opportunities are limited. Very often illegal drugs are introduced to Black youth at an early age which serve as a way to escape the pain of the experienced reality. Drug and alcohol abuse become rampant and many youth suffer from Post-Traumatic Stress Disorder (PSTD) as a consequence of living in the ghetto. Childhood Adversity often has a lifetime of negative consequences.

The Black community is effectively under attack and has been since its inception in America. This attack must stop. Systematic racism must end. The system must be restructured. We can eliminate crime in the United States if we reform the entire police system.

POLICE LEADERSHIP

Police should play an important and vital role in the United States to improve the quality of life in our communities. Law abiding citizens should not have to fear the police. Unfortunately, many citizens across the nation have lost confidence in the police. The nation has polarized into two separate camps. There are those who argue for police reform and those who seek to justify all police misconduct. Unfortunately, law enforcement agencies around the nation have moved toward militarization and away from community orientated policing.

At the core of the arguments for police reform is the need to replace the current police leadership that promotes the repression of citizens, suppression of First Amendment Rights, and seeks to militarize police agencies. There is no place for this type of police leadership in an enlightened society. Many of these individuals would just a soon murder our own citizens for control and to assert authority. They follow the old racist philosophy of destroying thousands of innocent Black people rather than letting one guilty one go free. This mentality must go.

The author observed a mixed group of Black, White, and Hispanic youth discussion, after they saw the 8 minute and 46 second video of the police murder of George Floyd and listening to police union leaders attempt to justify police misconduct. These young people see the hypocrisy and racism of these police leaders. There are many police officers and police leaders which welcome police reform, but the old guard are resistant to any meaningful reform. This old guard leadership must go. The nation cannot move forward until they are gone. We encourage them to retire, quit, and get out of the way of progress.

Police leadership must become educated about the history of policing in the United States and understand the role of systemic racism. Systematic racism must be eliminated.

Police must view all citizens as part of the American family and shed the us against them mentality. This new police leadership must be cultivated through education and dialogue. The American educational system has failed to educate U.S. citizens about the history of racism in the United States and racism's impact on the current system of law enforcement and criminal justice.

Many criminal justice scholars analyze the role of poverty, single parent families, lack of family structure, the absences of the church, and lack of education in crime and punishment. Few truly address the role of systemic racist in our nation having one of the highest incarceration rates in the world. This author has observed racist police and prosecutors bring criminal charges against Black men with no viable evidence and where the individual was, in all likelihood, simply not guilty. Racist judges allow the charges to remain and linger in an attempt to force a plea bargain or put the Defendant's life on hold sometimes for years while baseless charges are pending.

The author grew up in a Black neighborhood in Delaware where local police officers and prosecutors worked to begin a arrest record on Black children as early as possible to establish a record to assure later incarceration as adults and to eliminate them as competition for future jobs, college scholarships, and opportunities these law enforcement leaders deemed should be reserved for White children. In reality, these law enforcement officials were themselves criminals but there was no one there to prosecute them or hold them accountable.

A recent Harvard study showed that conservative judges were doling out sentences to Black Defendants sometimes two to three times high then given to White Defendants for nearly identical crimes. Not only is justice in America not blind, it often has an evil eye and malicious hand. How long should this conduct on the part of judges and law enforcement officials be expected to be allowed to continue before citizens take matters into their own hands?

Well disciplined and competent police leadership will promote a unifying police philosophy which embraces all citizens as fellow Americans. Enlightened leadership will become crime prevention driven and promote police reforms and a change from an arrest driven system to a crime prevention driven system. Enlightened leadership will recognize the training needs and the need to eradicate systemic racist. Police leadership must embrace the community, not just a powerful elite that promotes police repression of citizens.

There is major work to do to bring about meaningful police reform. Police leadership must become transformational and work toward a vision of a society without systemic racism.

The police role in the community is often said to be to protect and serve the citizens. Yet powerful police unions have been infiltrated by former and active Ku Klux Klan members, racist alt-right leaders, and racist conservatives. These union leaders and many racist rank and file members understand the historic role the police play in the suppression and oppression of the Black community. These union leaders and members are actively engaged in the suppression and oppression of the Black community to sustain the historic system of economic exploitation. These individuals willfully, maliciously, and corruptly engage in racial profiling, excessive use of force, and the murder of Black citizens.

The question has become how do we rid ourselves of these police union leaders and rank and file members who are intentionally postured against the Black community. We can hope to persuade the majority to vote them out and end the corrupt system. More likely government action will be required to bring about the needed changes. The only other alternative is action by the community.

New Paradigm of Policing

in the United States

Enlightened police systems are driven by crime prevention, not arrest, conviction, and incarceration. The U.S. police system developed in earnest after the U.S. Civil War which occurred from 1861-1865. After ten years at attempts of reconstruction, the system gave way to the racist elements of American society. States passed Black Codes or laws designed to suppress Black progress and continue the economic exploitation of Black communities. Law enforcement centered around finding any excuse to arrest and incarcerate Black men to place them in chain gangs and lease them to White landowners as cheap labor. The system spawned what many called kangaroo courts where corrupt judges worked with local landowners to supply cheap labor in the form of Black men convicted of petty crimes such as vagrancy, loitering, trespassing, and homelessness.

Legal separation of the races became the law of the land in the United States. Most law enforcement officials and officers were White males. These White male police officers targeted Black communities to meet arrest quotas to extract fines and fees from the Black community and to incarcerate Black males to supply cheap labor to White farmers. This is the foundation of policing in the United States. The system spawned the criminal justice system we have today.

After the U.S. Civil War Black people were freed from the bondage of slavery with no land or property to cultivate. Virtually everywhere they went was the property of others. If they went on someone else's land they would be charged with trespassing and put in chain gangs. If they remained on public highways or public lands they would be arrested for loitering or vagrancy and put in chain gangs. Since the Black community had few alternatives, many Blacks entered exploitive sharecropping arrangements with their former masters or other corrupt White landowners who were part of a corrupt system organized by local White landowners which later evolved into the Ku Klux Klan.

Establishing a new paradigm of policing in the United States requires us to acknowledge the corruption and corrupt roots of the current system. We will never make meaningful reforms unless we can recognize and repudiate the corruption of the current system. The current corrupt system has many supporters whose livelihoods are built upon this corrupt system. The police officers who racially profile Black citizens and commit police brutality and engage in corrupt practices, the judges who support the system, prison guards and criminal justice officials, and the prosecutors and lawyers who all benefit from the current system will resists change without a workable reform model.

The new paradigm of policing in the United States must have a unifying philosophy, be crime prevention driven, require major reforms in training and professional development, must include citizen and community involvement, and require a major change in union leadership and union model.

Unifying Philosophy

In Japan, the police unifying philosophy was unspoken but very clear and pronounced. Japanese police officers had a sense of national pride which made them view all citizens as members of a single Japanese family. Japanese police view themselves as part of the community with a personal responsibility for the development of the youth. Japanese police officers usually live in the community, actively participate in local community crime prevention councils, and spend a major portion of their time working directly with youth including teaching Karate, Judo, Jujitsu, Kendo, Aikido, and other martial arts and personal discipline systems.

Police officers in the United States usually do not live in the neighborhoods they are assigned to serve. They often view members of their own immediate family and children and youth who are close to them in their own family and neighborhood differently that the children and youth in the neighborhoods where they work as police officers. Police officer are more likely to provide youth diversion away from the criminal justice system for members of their own family and their friends and neighbors. Usually, they are outsiders when they are assigned to work and they view local citizens with a level of disdain which drives their indifference to the plight of local citizens, children, and youth in the communities they serve. They live by a double standard. On the one hand they work to save their own family and friends' children but seek to make and label Black children and other children of color in neighborhoods where they work under a corrupt model of policing.

The legacy of slavery, Jim Crow segregation, and the current system of discrimination have a current adverse impact on current police philosophy. Many police officers, police leaders, and police union officials view all Black youth as criminals or potential criminals. Most Black males in the United States have bad experiences with the police directly or have witnessed police harassment of other Black children and youth. This universal experience results in Black communities having an innate mistrust for the police. On the one hand, Black communities need the police but on the other hand Black communities see the police brutality and corruption which occurs daily.

New police leadership must emerge which recognized the contradictions in police philosophy and its internal inconsistencies. Police must be taught to view all United States citizens as part of a single family. Police officer training must result in police officers viewing all American children as members of their own family. Police agencies must operationalize this new police philosophy by shifting from an arrest driven model to a crime prevention model which focus on building the character and skills of our children and youth to help them become citizens in our communities which are contributing members of society.

Crime Prevention Driven

As a young teenage, the author recalls a personal experience walking home from school. A police patrol car passed by him and the two officers made eye contact with the author as they slowly rode past. The police patrol car stopped further up the street. The two officers jumped out in front of an abandoned house where a group of youth were gambling. The youth scattered and ran. The police gave chase, but all the youth got away. The author was on his way to his part-time job after school. The same two police officers rode up to the author further down the road, jumped out of their police vehicle, grabbed the author and slammed the author on the hood of the police cruiser and demanded the author give them the names of the youth who ran from them and got away. The author refused to give the police officer the names of any of the youth after having been mistreated by police. The next time the author had a similar experience, a police officer was injured while engaging in misconduct.

People in the community know the difference between right and wrong. Police create a hostile relationship with communities when they mistreat its youth. These corrupt police practices are so widespread throughout the United that most Black males you stop on the streets can tell you stories of their personal experience and victimization by this corruption.

The U.S. police system is rewarded for making arrest and solving crimes. District Attorney's Offices are driven by conviction rates. Judges are appointed or elected because they take a tough stand on crime and promise to send so-called criminals to prison. Jails and prisons do little to nothing to address mental health issues, poverty, lack of education, and underlying issues which drive crime. Lawyers are rewarded to pretend in the drama of due process. The system has become so corrupt that the U.S. Department of Justice studies show that many American cities racially profile Black citizens and Black communities to extract fines and fees and economically exploit Black communities. Local courts are participants in this Black exploitation. Most judges are more interested in supporting the corrupt system than making police officers accountable for corrupt practices. This system must change.

The federal government can lead police reform by changing the funding model for federal law enforcement funding assistance. Legislation is needed to shift the focus of federal law enforcement dollars to a crime prevention driven model of policing. Federal law enforcement dollars should be redirected to support crime prevention activities in local communities, re-train police officers, and reward youth diversion. There will also be bad actors who need to feel the will of the citizens. In Japan, one of the reasons crimes were so low in the 1980's is because citizens cooperated with police without hesitation. Citizens viewed police as inherently just. Citizen were never left to wonder if police would murder a youth from the neighborhood for a petty crime or if the police would empower youth in the community to retaliate against them and leave them unprotected.

Police Training

Many U.S. police officers are former military trained for combat in a hostile war zone or outright racist who view the Black community as needing control by an occupying force. Basic Law Enforcement Training in the United States does nothing to create a positive unifying police philosophy or prepare police officers to effectively work in poor and minority communities.

Police Officers in Japan were required to complete a 2-year police training program which included reasoning and thinking games, flower arrangement, cultural education, and character building. Police officers were required to be physically fit and self-confident. Police Officers were required to achieve a Black Belt level in martial arts personal discipline system such are Karate, Aikido, or Judo. Police Officers in Japan understand Japanese history and culture.

When a police officer was assigned to a neighborhood, the office became a part of the community. A fellow citizen. Police Officers helped to organize the local community and establish local crime prevention associations as part of a national crime prevention association. Police Officers were not driven by arrest but successful youth diversion. No arrest quotas liken often occurs in the United States.

In contrast to Japan, in the United States, police officers training consists of basic criminal law, firearms training, and a racially biased police philosophy. Basic Law Enforcement Training last about 6-months. The author observed that the basic difference in law enforcement in the United States and Japan which accounts for the differences in crime rates and incarceration rates is the level of training and professional standards of the frontline level police officer. The U.S. police officers are not trained or prepared to create a unifying American culture. In the United States, police are a part of a system of systemic racism and economic exploitation which has its roots in slavery and Jim Crow segregation.

U.S. Police Reform will require longer and better police training and professional development. New policing standards built upon a crime prevention model is required. The author observed multiple real life recording of police officer in action which resulted in the murder of Black citizens. One of the things which stood out the most is the U.S. police officers are driven by unreasonable fears which arise from the guilt that accompanies being a racist or being part of a system that tolerates overt racism. Police training and professional development must address the issue of racism in law enforcement. There is no place for racism in law enforcement.

Community Involvement

In Japan, a National Crime Prevention Association established as unified community. Communities take responsibility to provide positive activities for children and youth, and to promote their education and character development. Few young people choose crime because their communities provide them with many other positive choices. The responsibilities of police officers include organizing communities to help prevent crime.

On our visit to Japan in 1988, we observed operation of a program in one community in Osaka called the "Just Say Hello" Program. Citizens from the community, including the elderly, went out on the streets to just say hello to children and youth and any strangers in their neighborhood. They played board games with youth, taught them martial arts, basket weaving, arts and crafts, and directly engaged child and youth in positive relationships. People coming into a community were not likely to commit crime because of the level of vigilance of the community. People entering communities were treated with such a level of love and respect they would likely never even consider committing a crime in that neighborhood.

The nation and community's public health response was to view illegal drug usage and addiction as a public health crisis, not as crime. People were given mental health counseling, treatment, and support instead of being locked in jail or prison for drug usage or drug related crimes.

The level of training received by police officers in Japan prepared them to actively participate in helping communities fortify themselves against crime. Community safety consists of more than window locks, home security systems, and arresting people who commit crimes. In Japan community safety consisted of citizens making sure there was a place in the community for all its citizens and looking out for the health, safety, and well-being of others.

After visiting Japan in 1988, the author organized a group of Black men which included professionals, police officers, and regular working people to operate s Simba Program. "Simba" is a Ki Swahili word which means "Young Lions." Simba is a mentoring program and Rite of Passage designed to help Black youth transition into manhood. There is a female counterpart program called "Melaka." In Wilmington we organized about 75 men who served as mentors for Black children and youth age 8-16 years old. The passage lasted for one year. Each week we met with our Simba's and conducted life-skills training which including a curriculum with topics ranging from "use of credit and personal finances" to "avoiding street gang culture." Each month we took a field trip to a place of cultural and historic significance such as the Museum of African Art. Black owned businesses hosted events for the Simba youth which included fun activities and education designed to prepare them for the real world. We took a camping trip and had use of the Delaware National Guard Training Site at

Bethany Beach. We provided the Simba youth with martial arts training, a physical training obstacle course, and had a exciting and disciplined experience which was life changing for many of the Simba youth participants. The program culminated at the end of the year with a ceremony were the Simba youth received awards, a special hat and shirt which symbolized the year of passage. We then had a feast in their honor.

The Wilmington City Police Department allowed the Simba Program access to its facilities and many Black police officers served a volunteers and mentors for the program. This program became possible only after the city hired is first Black Police Chief, Samuel Pratcher, and Community Director, Pete Hickman. There were several police officers who played key roles to helping the program achieve success. The program was funded in part by a Public Health Grant for one year. The author served as the Executive Director of the Juvenile Awareness Education Program, Inc., which was the sponsoring agency. Jamie Lane, now Dr. Jamie Lane, served as the Simba Program Director. Simba was an effective crime prevention model but instead of supporting it, some the racist elements in the state created competitive grants to support mentoring programs which were not directly connected to the communities which needed such programs. All the funding went to programs in higher income neighborhoods. Systemic racism once again reared its ugly head.

Facilitating community involvement in crime prevention must become an important part of the funding model for law enforcement. The old hardliners must move out the way for enlightened leadership. The old hardliners have had their day and what they did has not worked well.

Leadership Changes

Wherever you see blatant police misconduct and police brutality you see police union leadership speaking out in resistance to police reform or attempting to justify obvious police misconduct and murders. These leaders have lost any moral authority they had in the face of the 8 minute and 46 second video showing the recent police murder of George Floyd. Police unions work to protect police officers who commit obvious misconduct. Police union leaders have created a climate in the United States where police officers feel empowered to openly commit crimes against American citizens because they feel protected and shielded by their police union leaders. The is no place for police unions in our society. Police unions are anti-theatical to positive police community relations. Police unions protect police from being held accountable for misconduct toward citizens in the community.

Police unions must be abolished or reformed by leadership which promotes a community policing philosophy. After the author's visit to Japan in 1988, the Delegation and the Milton S. Eisenhower Foundation promoted a national "Community Orientated Policing" Program. The U.S. Congress provided special funding to local law enforcement agencies to operate "Community Orientated Policing" programs across the nation. Many of the local police agencies sponsored Police Athletic Leagues and other local programs but most simply used the money to continue with repressive tactics and continue to harass Black youth or falsely give Black youth gang labels. For example, in Greenville, North Carolina local police claimed the existence of over 100 street gangs. The author worked for over five years in the same community and never encountered as single actual street gang. The police simply lied about street gangs to obtain federal funding. It was a common practice of local law enforcement agencies.

The current crop of conservative police union leaders has an us against them mentality. They view themselves as an occupying force in Black communities and communities of color. They support repression of the local populations and their conduct make these communities even more unsafe. The culture they create within police agencies penalizes police officers who would hold fellow officers accountable for misconduct and corruption. They encourage officers to look away when some bad apples engage in corrupt acts.

We must work to eliminate police unions for reform them. We must start by removing current police union leaders who promote repression of the community and attempt to excuse police misconduct.

POLICE EDUCATION AND TRAINING

Basic Law Enforcement Training for police officers in the United States consists of about 6-months of training before police officers work in communities and directly with citizens in response to 911 emergency calls. Police training in the United States is woefully inadequate. Officers learn to shoot, basic criminal law, driving, police chase, basic investigation, and use of force principles. Most training programs use a curriculum which teach officers that if a Black male looks in the officer's eyes the Black man is being confrontational and poses an immediate threat. Officers are taught that White males who look into the officer's eyes are simply attempting to communicate. Police officers' training literally teach them to be biased against Black males and other minority groups in initiating a use of force continuum. This teaching has resulted in the death of many Black males at the hands of the police because the police officer held a false belief about Black males which is a racist stereotype.   Many Black parents teach their children to look people in the eye when you speak to them as a sign of respect.

Basic Law Enforcement Training for police must be expanded to 2-years or more. The curriculum must be reformed to include culturally responsible policing, effective communication skills, community organizing, non-violent self-defense techniques, and problems solving and reasoning skills training. Police must be prepared to address mental health related issues and drug/alcohol addiction as public health issues. Police training must produce well-rounded individuals and not the modern stereotypical police officers who is a borderline alcoholic with repressed feels and who is not a well-adjusted human being.

Many of the people police encounter are not criminal they have mental health problems, are on drugs, or suffering from trauma in their lives. This is a public health crisis. In the United States we have used the police to address a public health crisis for which the police are not properly trained or prepared. Police training must prepare police officers on the street to address these issues without the use of excessive force.

Police training and education must prepare police officers to capture a vision of a harmonious community and the job must be transformed into building a harmonious community. Police officers should be educated about the history of the nation, both the good and the bad. A new vision must not hide Americas past but from its ashes build a better tomorrow. We all must learn from the missteps of the past.

We cannot continue to up misfits on the streets with guns and badges. We have people with histories of being racist or who have committed misconduct in other police departments who can simply just go get a job in another police department and continue to abuse citizens. There needs to be a national registry to prevent abusive officers from move from one jurisdiction to another. The amount and quality of professional training must be elevated.

In Japan, for example, police are required to achieve at least a Black Belt level in a martial arts form which teaches personal discipline. A person with a Black Belt is less likely to become undisciplined in a confrontation. In the United States, many police officers fear because they are weak individuals with no tradition of personal discipline. They are more likely to pull their guns when there is no real threat to their person or the person of others.

When we go back and examine the excessive force cases, most would have had different outcomes had the officers had a higher quality of training and professional standards. Some of the cases we see are simply police malpractice. The system is broken and needs to be fixed.

The case of Chris Darner is an important case study. Darner, a military veteran, reported police misconduct by a fellow officer.

Instead of the police department taking action to eliminate misconduct by officers, like a criminal street gang the police took action against Darner for "snitching" on a fellow officer. They ruined Darner's career. Darner retaliated by attacking police officers and their families. This type of retaliation against officers who demand high standards for police in common.

Another case of importance is the case of Mark Essex. Essex experience racial discrimination while in the U.S. Navy. Later, after police shot two Black students during student civil rights demonstrations Essex took to the roof tops to shoot police officers whom he deemed the enemies of the people.

Unprofessional and improperly trained police officers allowed on the streets have the potential to create a major backlash from citizens who are simply sick and tired of the racism and exploitation. About 29% of active duty military are Black females and 17% are Black males. What message is sent to them when we witness race-based executions against Black citizens by police. The military fight to protect the people from foreign enemies. What is the come to realize the racially motivated police officer are attacking Black Americans with impunity.

Education and training are important components of the American police system. We can no longer give racist a badge and a gun and set them on the streets. We must require police officers to at least be working toward a Bachelors Degree and receive at least two year of professional training with a reformed curriculum before a police officer is qualified to serve on the street.

NATIONAL CRIME PREVENTION

The United States needs a coherent national policy on the prevention of crime. The U.S. Congress needs to set crime prevention priorities and provide adequate crime prevention funding. Improved and increase training and professional development must be made mandatory for police. Citizens crime prevention must be promoted and expanded at the national and local levels.

National crime prevention is not solely the responsibility of police. It is a shared community responsibility. We reduce crime when our society is functioning more efficiently as a whole. Improvements in housing, education, employment, health care, and other aspects of American society directly impact crime.

We must develop programs across the nation which address the underly issues which impact and promote crime in our communities.

The first issue must be the elimination of systematic racism and the exploitation of the Black community. The system must become prevention driven and not continue to be driven by arrest and incarceration rates.

Local communities must be provided funding to organize locally to prevent crime. Local communities should be provided resources to provide positive activities for children and youth. Funds should support mentoring, martial arts training, chess clubs, sports and athletic training, and other positive activities in our communities. Schools must also eliminate systemic racism.

About 80 percent of teachers are white females. The out of school suspension rates of Black male students is off the charts. White females are not equipped to be effective teachers of Black children without special culturally responsive teacher training. The results we see are major achievement gaps between Black and White students. Public schools have become school-to-prison pipelines. We know this does not have to be because we have examples of public charter schools like Success Academies where poor Black children outperform elite White students on standardized test.

The system is broken and requires a massive overhaul. Crime prevention must center around empowering the community to take charge and become responsible for motivating Black youth and guiding them on a path of progressive progress.

The existing system has failed Black children and youth, and the Black community. The Black community must be empowered. A national crime prevention act which provides funding to local communities, which is not controlled by police, is urgently needed.

Black citizens should not have to fear police and its own youth. Police help create the conditions which exits which result in Black communities fearing both police and their own youth. The current system must be dismantled.

A national crime prevention association without a racist mentality is needed to help organize local communities under a new model which is crime prevention driven. Local communities must build the kinds of relationships with local children and youth which provides guidance that places children and youth on a path of progressive progress.

We can explore several options of program models and structure, but details are beyond the scope of this writing. A national non-profit organization should serve as an umbrella group and provide subgrants to local chapters or local independent groups. National sports figures should support these groups. The local groups should sponsor the organization of public charter schools to take charge of public education and empower local communities to provide for the education of students. Accountability systems should shut down charter schools that do not serve the interest of the community and perform better than local traditional public schools.

Police officers should be prohibited by law from unionizing. A police officer should be professionally licensed subject to professional standards set by state law and by professional licensing boards. Police officers' roles should include helping organize local communities to implement crime prevention measures which go well beyond home security systems, door locks, and community watch programs. Real crime prevention must include mentoring youth, providing organized youth activities, tutoring, and raising the educational standards.

Local crime prevention groups need to be empowered and provided a vision which inspires and motivates them to improve the quality of life in our communities. We can no longer sit back because of fear of the police and local authorities. Local communities must be empowered. It is now well demonstrated that the old system which is systematically racist has not worked. We need a new way forward which improves the quality of life for all.

It is not necessarily required that the system be uniform. We could implement different organizational structures in different regions of the nation to determine which will work best.

REFORMING THE CRIMINAL JUSTICE SYSTEM

Our discussion of police reform must expand to include major criminal justice reform. We must change the roles of prisons, courts, prosecutors, and lawyers in the criminal justice system. Our focus in this writing has been on police reform but these other components of the system need reform too. These systems are also infected with systematic racism.

Most poor people and Black people have had enough experience with the criminal justice system to recognize that justice in America is a myth. The courts administer disparate sentences to whites and blacks for the same crimes even if the individual defendants have similar backgrounds. Racism is so overt it cannot be hidden any longer. Blacks are disproportionately imprisoned for similar crimes and there is no plausible explanation except racial bias by judges and court personnel involved in developing sentencing recommendations.

Prisons warehouse Black people at alarming rates. Prison recidivism directly correlates to the lack opportunity for education and training of prisoners. Prisons promote negative values in prisoners and push prisoners toward future misconduct by releasing prisoner who are now a little older, with greater responsibilities, and less preparation to carry out their responsibilities. It's like intentionally pushing people in prison toward a path of future failure.

Conservative groups have pushed for more conservative judges because conservative judges have proved to be harsher on Black defendants than White defendants, according to a recent Harvard Study. Its overly racist. If you have racist judges, who can have confidence in the judicial system? The system must reform or its will ultimately be dismantled by the people.

Prosecutors and Defense lawyers are supposed to represent the interest of the people and the individual defendants and ensure that due process occurs. Unfortunately, due process is becoming more illusion than reality when the bail system assures the poor defendants go immediately to jail while more affluent defendant are released on bail and can often buy their cases with money by paying high priced lawyers.

The system has become so corrupt the people are losing confidence in the system as a whole. Unless there is reform soon it is difficult to imagine there not being a complete breakdown of the entire system.

The U.S. Department of Justice Study of the police pattern and practice in the City of Ferguson Missouri showed that the local courts are complicit with local law enforcement in racially profiling and economically exploiting the Black community. The Study showed the courts were more interested in raising revenues for the city than they were interested in justice or holding police officers accountable for misconduct against Black citizens.

The Trump administration has taken away the façade of decency. Corruption is open and bare. Police have been encouraged to use excessive force by the President. The President has threatened violence against protestors seeking to demand the government change its practices and end systemic racism.

America is at a crossroads. We must develop the will and manifest the intelligence to change and reform the system. The United States is a young nation. It has its faults, but we must learn from the mistakes and not seek to repeat them. Police reform can make our nation better for all its citizens. We should look at the positive benefits of establishing a new paradigm for police and criminal justice. The model should be prevention driven. As a nation, we must also address the issue of Reparations, housing, health care, education, employment, and other aspects of our society which are vital to the success of a nation.

It is sheer incompetence and mismanagement when our cities go up in flames because our govern has abused the people. The people act in desperation when they are abused and have nothing to lose. As a nation, we should never place the people in the position where they have to protest, riot, or burn down cities to get their point across.

POLICE REFORM AND FEDERAL FUNDING

The United States Congress provides federal funding to state and local police agencies each year. Congress, through legislation, can tie federal funding to police reform. Congress can shift the law enforce focus to crime prevention and support the organization of crime prevention groups in community through a legislative initiative and spending legislation. The issue is whether Congress will shift its priorities.

The existing system operates with the support and blessings of Congress. Congress must accept that things must change and adopt police reform legislation. Congress could shift priority to crime prevention, it could include mandatory increased training and professional development in spending bills, and it could fund crime prevention community groups if it chooses to do so.

Congress could require the Bureau of Justice Statistics to shift its focus or add new data collection categories to include crime prevention activities and report progress on this new initiative.

We always hear about the numbers of crimes committed and the numbers of arrest. We hear about the number of people incarcerated. We rarely hear about activities that are part of a crime prevention initiative. We must change our national mentality about crime and punishment. Our success should not be measured in arrest, convictions, and incarceration. Our success should be measured by lower crime rates. Local communities should be rewarded for low crime rates.

Federal funds should support youth activities, improve education, provide job training, support the development of local businesses, improve housing conditions, and make the community a better place for children to grow up and families to thrive and experience success.

Congress should require all persons incarcerate to complete a high school diploma or master a trade in prison. Prison should not be a revolving door. It should be a time to restore the individual incarcerated and reconcile them back to the community as a productive member of society.

Congress should tie federal funding for courts to mandatory training for prosecutors, defense attorneys, and judges. These officials must be re-educated to understand the history and reality of systemic racism and a new national vision to eliminate it.

Finally, Congress should adopt a timetable to implement police reforms. Within three to five years local police agencies should be required to make needed reforms and implement training and professional development. All new officer should be required to complete the two-year training programs.

CONCLUSION

This book is a call to action. The community must go well beyond discussions of defunding the police. We must talk about major police reform and what it should look like. The author has discussed the Japanese model and shared thoughts about police reform. A crime prevention driven system of police reform is desperately needed at this time in history.

The Black community has been the target of economic exploitation since the founding of the nation. While some progress has been made, systemic racism permeates the system and demands immediate reform.

Not only must police reform, but the entire criminal justice system must reform. Reparations for Black Americans must include reforms to the police and criminal justice systems. The way forward is the elimination of systemic racism.

ABOUT THE AUTHOR

OZIE LEE HALL, JR. was born in Wilmington, Delaware in the 1950's. At the age of five years old he witnessed the Ku Klux Klan burn a cross in front of his parent's house. Rev. Hall has experienced police brutality and the criminal justice system first-hand. He is a long-time advocate of Reparation for the Black community. Rev. Hall is the author of the book: Reparations: The Healing of America. Rev. Hall is an educational advocate. This book was written to stimulation positive discussion with the goal of achieving police reform.

BIBLIOGRAPHY

Bayley, D. (1991). *Forces of Order: Policing Modern Japan.* Los Angeles: University of California Press.

Curtis, L. A. (1974). *Criminal Violence: National Patterns and Behavior.* Lexington: Lexington Books.

Curtis, L. A. (2018). *Healing Our Divided Society.* Philadelpha: Temple University Press.

Division, U. D. (2015). *Investigation of the Ferguson Police Department.* Washington, D.C.: U.S. Department of Justice.

Division, U. D. (2016). *Investigation of the Baltimore City Police Department.* Washington, D.C.: USDOJ.

Fannon, F. (1961). *The Wretched of the Earth.* New York: Grove Press.

Hall, O. L. (2019). *Reparations: The Healing of America.* Spring Lake: Advanced Education Systems Publishing.

Harris, D. A. (2020). *Racial Profiliing: Past, Present, and Future?* Washington, D.C.: American Bar Association.

Higginbotham, A. L. (1996). *Shades of Freedom.* London: Oxford University Press.

Higginbothan, A. L. (1980). *In the Matter of Color: Race and the American Legal Process.* London: Oxford University Press.

J.M. Horowitz, A. B. (2019). *Race in America 2019.* New York: Pew Research Center.

Roland G. Fryer, J. (2016). *An Empirical Analysis of Racial Differences in Police Use of Force.* Boston: Harvard University.

Silberman, C. (1978). *Criminal Violence Criminal Justice.* New York.

Wolfgang, M. (1990). Crime and Punishment in Renassiance Florence. *Journal of Criminal Law and Criminology*, 81(3); 567-84.